Truda's Double Dose

By

Andrea Burke

Hosur, krishnagiri district ,
Tamil Nadu,
India - 635 109

Email:and_freelance@Yahoo.com
2023 - *Andrea Burke*

BLUEROSE PUBLISHERS
India | U.K.

Copyright © Andrea Burke 2023

All rights reserved by author. No part of this publication may be reproduced, stored in a retrieval system or transmitted in any form or by any means, electronic, mechanical, photocopying, recording or otherwise, without the prior permission of the author. Although every precaution has been taken to verify the accuracy of the information contained herein, the publisher assumes no responsibility for any errors or omissions. No liability is assumed for damages that may result from the use of information contained within.

BlueRose Publishers takes no responsibility for any damages, losses, or liabilities that may arise from the use or misuse of the information, products, or services provided in this publication.

For permissions requests or inquiries regarding this publication, please contact:

BLUEROSE PUBLISHERS
www.BlueRoseONE.com
info@bluerosepublishers.com
+91 8882 898 898
+4407342408967

ISBN: 978-93-5989-471-3

First Edition: November 2023

Foreword

As a part-time teacher, I had never dreamt of writing a book..When thoughts overflow, penning words into poems becomes a desirable art. My family showed me their love in various ways.

" <u>Truda's Simple Doses</u> " (35 poems) was published in June and <u>"Truda's Double Dose"</u> (65 poems) is another one to publish in 2023. Hence,this "Double Dose" includes various types of poems like freestyle, sestain, haikus, tankas, diamante, +ing ballads, triolet, cinquains and so on….

A little fun and twist , good positive vibes to sad outcomes, spreading goodness, showing true love, being open and honest in communication, enjoying nature and regaining joy to reduce stress are included in this anthology.

There are wounds that none can identify yet it bleeds,then,taking time and efforts to show empathy will help overcome anything.The process of aging or losing lives isn't easy in life yet the hope is for a BETTER Life which is soon ahead…

Reading is as patient as Love is.. <u>Art can open a heart too</u>…

May we always praise the creator for our talents!

May you respect and read my contents!

Contents

1. Respect 1
2. Pure Rain 2
3. Color Poem "Burgundy" 3
4. Lemon Extract 4
5. Two and Two Will Continue 5
6. Enthusiasm 6
7. My Eyes, My Tears 7
8. The Sapling 9
9. It Is Usual To Feel Unusual 10
10. Not All Wounds Bleed 11
11. A Mind's Kit 12
12. The Scream and the Laughter 13
13. Unique 14
14. The cycle of seasons 15
15. Heaped in the empty desert 16
16. The Take Aways 17
17. Calculating Time 18
18. Empty Speech 19
19. A Flimsy Paper 20
20. A Flash of Views 21
21. A Keyhole 22
22. An Ice-Cube 23

23. Anxiety 24
24. Love Is Solid Gold 25
25. Am I Helpless? 26
26. Siblings 27
27. In Dismay 28
28. A Pit 29
29. Losing a Loved One 30
30. A Lovely Catalog 31
31. Heal and feel 32
32. Nothing More Than Loyalty 33
33. It isn't easy 34
34. Love, In Effect, Is Love 35
35. Daughter 36
36. A Knack 37
37. Who Could Fix A Broken Heart? 38
38. A midget 39
39. The Timely Effort 40
40. Reduce Stress 41
41. Peace and War 42
42. The Pine (Tree) and My Spine 43
43. What You Can Rob 44
44. Singleness 45
45. An Open Ear 46
46. Rip me not 47
47. Mother's Love 48
48. I Blink, Think And Sink 49

49. In a jovial mood 50
50. Spread Goodness 51
51. From A Drop To The Last Word 52
52. Serum 53
53. A Pleasant Start in the Park 54
54. A True Love Seed 56
55. The Best Satisfaction 57
56. Time Is Precious 58
57. Crab Curry Recipe 59
58. Ollie- The Baby Elephant 60
59. An Art 61
60. A Splash 62
61. A fruitful tree 63
62. An Exceptionally Large Ocean 64
63. Struggles within 65
64. Yearning to be unlocked 66
65. A Complete 100 67

1. Respect

The one

    who values

        Your value

            is a person

                of high value.

Respect Her !

    Respect Him !

2. Pure Rain

I look up at the sky,
I gaze at the aurora,
Ah! I feel soothing,
I sense the dewy petrichor,
Then the breeze blows...
Plonk! Drops a drop of rain,
On my cheek.
And then the downpour:
Washing away worries.

I step into the water,
To enjoy the moment.
I dance in awe:
In the stagnant muddy puddle.

A sensation of an ice-cream in the palate.
Yipee! How delighted!
Are you a real pluviophile?

If pure rain is life to the soil,
The treasured feeling is novel.

3. Color Poem "Burgundy"

Burgundy is a pretty, bold and beautiful color,
Burgundy smells like pleasant calla lily and orchids,
Burgundy tastes like delicious wine,
Burgundy looks like shiny, coloring hair creme,
Burgundy sounds like a cracking of a butterfly,
Burgundy feels like smooth, elegant, silky gown,
Burgundy makes me feel relaxed and peaceful.

4. Lemon Extract

Love that springs a slander
Is like a colander
Full of holes
Always strolls
Never to hold
Forever to grow cold
Like licked cream
Between the wafers
With high velocity
Seldom with felicity
Ends up brooding
Needs much pruning
Like opposite poles
Only to attract
Rarely a pure lemon extract.

5. Two and Two Will Continue

To argue, it needs two,
Argumenting into two and two,
Never leads to a proper view,
Melt, refine, and relish yourselves like a Fondue.

#Fondue- a lovely dish

6. Enthusiasm

*Enthusiasm is

A contagious sickness that elevates the joy—

*A Haiku- Enthusiasm is a positive quality

7. My Eyes, My Tears

My eyes
Glisten with tears,
My tears
Receive it as souvenirs,

                                  Read its meaning within its spheres,
                                          It stings within my eyeball,
                                              It burns like a fireball,
                                            Shedding it on my bed,
                                            Soaking every thread;

Beads rolling down my cheeks,
Stretch your palms;
Collect it through all the weeks,
It grips and lifts you with psalms,

                                  Never does it toss like a tidal wave,
                                        Flowing tears can hideaway,
                                        Save it as modern antique:
                                            Feel it's dampness,
                                            Taste the saltiness,

May it improve Knowledge ,
Like tongue twitters ,
My tears are precious pebbles,
Connecting rivers,

> *I wish I could fill an empty dam;*
> *When it opens the gate again,*
> *Reach it's flow,*
> *Wash your face and feel cool..*

How can I hold my tears back again!
Who can stop my tears?

> *For we come from the womb,*
> *We shed tears,*
> *For we go to the tomb,*
> *We shed fears,*

Dear me! How comforting it is to know that sorrows will soon pass away!
Tearless life soon to go away in Paradise!

8. The Sapling

The withered sapling

I see it sad and droopy

Hiding from my smile

9. It Is Usual To Feel Unusual

Lips can't speak
Eyes can't see
Ears can't ear
Limbs can't walk
Touch feels numb
Tongue goes wrong
Trachea doesn't digest
I am without strength
I can't get along
I can't stretch my arm,
How can I fix it's joint
What is pain that becomes
every part of the body!

This is usual to feel unusual;
Jeez! This is unusual.

10. Not All Wounds Bleed

Wounds are fresh,
Who could do anything to refresh?

I can't remove even a pound of flesh,
The platelets fail to be like a mesh,

I don't know how to care for my wound,
Not even an ultrasound can find how profound,

Some say, "Oh! It's better" on seeing the scabs on the outside,
yet it doesn't seem to heal inside,

Not all wounds bleed !
Not all wounds bleed !

11. A Mind's Kit

My thoughts keep worrying me,
Discern it a bit.

Worried thoughts keep triggering me sourly,
Peep into that kit.

Triggered thoughts keep inspiring me untimely,
It's still safe in a locket.

Search for it deeply,
You'll find it in your pocket.

12. The Scream and the Laughter

The scream
Loud, anguished
Piercing, crying, yelling
Sadness, pain, regret, moody

Ease, contentment
Calming, entertaining, soothing
Joyful, peppy
The laughter

A Diamante- ◊

13. Unique

Love for the significant other stays for ages,
As empathy and sympathy interchanges,
It doesn't search for a selfish purpose,
It is complete, dedicated, earnest in surplus.

14. The cycle of seasons

Love the rain before
The fall , right after a fall—
Blossom then rise to
Shine — Love the routine of life
Like the cycle of seasons

 # A Tanka poem

15. Heaped in the empty desert

Deserted in the barren land,
She walks on the hot dry sand,

In the scorching heat,
Wishing for good things to be heaped,

What can she do to enhance?
Yeet! Her feet wishes to tap-dance,

While being near her beloved,
His pure love flows in her blood.

16. The Take Aways

I scream you scream,
Would it taste like ice cream ?
Oh ! The take away doesn't fade away,
Let's decide to get back right away.

17. Calculating Time

From seconds to minutes,
From minutes to hours,
From moments to memories,
I calculate my precious time spent,

Adding happiness and Joy,
Multiplying no worries,
Diving every fears,
Subtracting nothing in Love,

How precious time is !
How precious time is !

18. Empty Speech

A crow caws ca ca ,
Peeking away leftovers,
Lazy as ever,
So is an imprudent man's
Flummoxed empty speech – flares You!

🔊 🔉 🔈

 # A Tanka poem

19. A Flimsy Paper

Like paper use me
Not- to ink your thoughts down then
To squeeze me out when
Your mind satisfies itself
Tear me not into pieces.

✂✉

A Tanka poem

20. A Flash of Views

I flash my views,
As a flash of lightning,
But many to refuse,
The pressure tightening,

I get puzzled,
I try to figure out a way,
Like paddling a kayak, I struggled ;
At long last, I made my day without delay.

21. A Keyhole

You peeped into my life as through a keyhole,
I made every effort to play a unique role,
Under my tent, I kept you safe to support as a tent-pole,
After my loss, who would console?

> # A tragic situation !

22. An Ice-Cube

Your soothing words run deep
Into my thoughts; Seek ;
As if an ice-cube
Rolling down my cheek,

You! I never fooled,
Only stooped to soothe
Your raw, itchy
Persisting wound.

I wish I could freeze you in an ice-cube,
Improving my mood,
Not allowing any heat wave,
To melt you down,

Be not an ice-floe,
That would slowly float
Or be pushed over yet grow
Large as an ice-sheet.

23. Anxiety

Anxiety

    Eating

        Worrying

Fearing

    Trembling

        Depressing

Panicking

        # – ing poem

24. Love Is Solid Gold

Love is solid gold,
however, Impure love is dried grass,
Love is impressive and expressive,
It is never hesistant yet evident, also persistent,

Love is like a calm sea that helps survival,
If disturbed by any uncertainty,
Becomes rough or turbulent,
For we wish to sail on the same boat,

Love never mends and knows how to fend,
Fascinatingly, it grows stronger and stronger.
Hope is True that real Love is Solid gold!
However, impure motives are dried grass.

25. Am I Helpless?

Am I helpless?

                        It is obvious that I feel hopeless.

I am deeply apprehensive;

                        Could it have been a little comprehensive?

I was bashful and boastful,

                        Soon after, I refused to be resentful or regretful.

                    # A Sestain
    # Negative feelings can get you down. Don't give up!

26. Siblings

As creepers, climbers

So are sisters and brothers

Walking hand in hand—

27. In Dismay

The white clouds turn gray,
That's when emotions can't portray,
I can't stand but sway,
Everything fills me in great dismay.

A Ballad quatrain

28. A Pit

The cold winds can't blow our love,
Neither the scorching sun melt it,
Nor the waves flow through us,
Only if you dump me in a pit.

A Ballad quatrain

29. Losing a Loved One

She couldn't bear the loss
Of his death, Oh Love!
He left her with two beautiful children,
To call her own,
For her to make their way,
On becoming anxious,
This way or that way,
Which way?
She wondered and wondered !

Finally, she found a way,
That helped them stay,
Possibly it could be the right way;
May be God's way,
She believes that the way
Leads them to Paradise.

Eagerly waiting to receive
The lost loved one on the way,
This way leads to Paradise!

30. A Lovely Catalog

You make me understand with every look,
We could fill our images in a comic book.

Reading over and over again every dialog,
Collecting all details in a catalog.

Protecting ourselves from any harm using a bullet proof,
Whereas Life's lessons can build our golden roof.

A Sestain

31. Heal and feel

No jokes break a bone-

Jealousy makes it rotten-

Heal — feel content, calm !

32. Nothing More Than Loyalty

In life, whatever we do with liberty,
We want to get through with dignity,

Why be hasty?
Let's not make anything weighty.

Can't we make it to our eighties ?
For better, changing our personalities,

Trying to be steady even when shaky,
In Love! Not Feeling thirsty,

Together! We are worthy,
Understand that there is nothing more than loyalty,

Nothing is more than loyalty!
Oh Wow! That is the best royalty !

33. It isn't easy

Rupturing of a seed coat,
Sheeding of a snake's skin,

Treating a dreadful disease,
Healing a hurt soul,

Allowing emotions to paralyze oneself,
Repairing a lovely lost bond,

Facing everyday's struggles alone,
Aging and feelings of being a burden,

Losing a beloved one to death,
Nothing is easy in life.

Nothing is easy in life,
If it's easy, it never remains in life.

It isn't easy!
It isn't easy!

34. Love, In Effect, Is Love

Love connects the hearts,
Interlocks thoughts and emotions,
Projects pure motives,
Directs the path of life.

Even if it hurts, it forgives,
Sincere love heals any pain of grief
Which is the most painful emotions;
Hence, it gives relief.

Love from the heart is a tonic
That aids in recovery,
Even from the deepest wounds,
Truly, Love, in effect, is love

Love gives no way to doubts,
But preserves cute, little, crazy moments.
Truly, Love is, in effect, love

35. Daughter

Daughter
    Caring
Supporting
    Sympathizing
Comforting
    Entertaining
Hard-working
    Respecting
Performing
    Resisting

36. A Knack

To talk to people with a knack,
To help them get onto their track,
Serves a perfect snack,
Like a gift-pack.

> \# *Fighting against odds to do Good to people in small doses is rewarding*

37. Who Could Fix A Broken Heart?

Who could fix a broken heart?
Eventually, I'm trying harder to restart,

It's more painful than fixing a broken bone,
because I don't know how it is torn,

I wish I could call the doctor to treat,
I'm dreadful and unsteady on my feet,

Finally, I call out to the Greatest Doctor,
Who resides in the heavens to care for me softer.

38. A midget

A little midget —

Sights everything to fidget

Brings it all to me

A Haiku
Little Infants/ Babies are adorable

39. The Timely Effort

Walk to talk ,
Walk and talk ,
Talk not for being fought
But to adjust an anxious thought,
With a little forethought,

When the living is dead,
One can neither walk nor talk,
A little effort is worth,
The timely effort.

40. Reduce Stress

Driving on the road

Influences our mood ------ well !

Helps focus —— not stress

41. Peace and War

To have peace within, there is war between my mind and my heart,
None can predict what ,
Truth doesn't know what to fake,
It doesn't know what to break.

42. The Pine (Tree) and My Spine

I see the yellow dust on the pine,
Likewise, I feel the gray and white matter in my spine,

The pollen grains cling to the cone,
while, the little disks bridge my bone,

It's more valuable for its timber,
Yet, I manage a weary smile and fall into a peaceful slumber,

It's cones are collected for proteins and spread on the yard,
While, I receive various messages through the spinal cord,

Oh Creator! What a beautiful evergreen Pine(tree) !
Oh Creator! How wise you are to curve my Spine !

43. What You Can Rob

You can rob
Not just valuable
things
Of someone
But also their
Real love
And
Real worth
Which no hidden
Cameras could
Ever detect.

44. Singleness

Singleness, sincere , sharp
Independant, Integrity well-balanced
Noble, notable
Grateful, giggling ones
Lasting Friendships
Expressive, empathetic deeds
Neat, Non-violent
Easygoing, earnest, elegant
Serene, steadfast in everything
Single by choice or by circumstances yet productive

#Acrostic poem

45. An Open Ear

If I go into space with you,
Breaking through complete darkness,
That would be light years.
How lovely to talk with an Open Ear!

46. Rip me not

A bond so profound-

Responds and corresponds like

A *covalent bond

> # A Haiku

* A covalent bond is referred to as a strong chemical bond.

47. Mother's Love

Mother, You are like a huge tree,
You extend your love to our needs,
Doing everything for us without our plea,
Always showing love happily.

48. I Blink, Think And Sink

I blink blink until —

I think think think of you and

Sink Sink into You

Haiku

49. In a jovial mood

Love evaluates and rekindles only true Love,
Love forgets nothing good,
It rejects every malice,
It keeps the family in a jovial mood.

50. Spread Goodness

The sun wakes up early
Smiles on people
Scatters a short wavelength
To reach far beyond.

Likewise,

A faithful woman whose
Small doses of true love
In word and in deed
Eventually spreads
Goodness in her family

Being sincere and trying to get along,
Prolongs the unity in the family.

51. From A Drop To The Last Word

A drop of water is life's gem,
Drop by drop trickles from a stem,

Like beads of pearls,
It fills the beautiful earth's reserves,

The last drop of water quenches a thirst,
Makes one feel like a baby being nursed,

A drop is also a life's fall,
Filling life with a lot of troubles,

It makes me feel small,
How amazing to receive an immediate call!

Every reassured repeated last word,
Can make a better change in life afterward.

52. Serum

To nourish your hair,
Keeping away every tear,

To brighten your skin,
Feeling the aroma of a Jasmine,

To repair a damage,
Gradually improving its fruitage.

Lovely Serum!
In melody, there is a constant hum!

53. A Pleasant Start in the Park

Eagerly approaching the park,
Oh! How pleasant a day to spark!

Early in the morning,
All heads are nodding,

While walking on the track,
Happily sighting no trap,

For a while, I sit on a smooth stone,
Keeping aside the phone,

I view a lovely lake,
Thanking the creator for everyday's awake;

The dazzling seiche of the lake is fascinating,
This basin between the road and the rail is admiring,

I glance at the beauty of the flowers on the trees
Discerning it's marvelous varieties,

How adorable is the striking bright green Beetle!
How it loves to eat the flowers little by little!

We find many ways to appreciate,
The creation and to take time to meditate.

54. A True Love Seed

A true love seed was found
Before it could be rooted;
In the fertile soil,
It was carried off from
Dry soil to damp soil
Red soil to brown soil,
It felt it could produce,
Fruitage everywhere,

It is still above the soil,
Unable to find a place anywhere,
It seems an unproductive dispersal whereas
Aiding it to germinate
Turns us to enjoy its rich heritage.

#Trueloveseed is a real seed that grows into a medicinal plant

55. The Best Satisfaction

When We find real friends to associate,
It saves us from a narrow escape,
When we receive unselfish love, care and compassion,
Imagine! How it brings us the best satisfaction!

56. Time Is Precious

Time is precious,
We wish to be gracious,

Although, We know the exact time,
People come into our life anytime,

Time is defined as temporary,
Yet exists permanently,

Time matters for many,
Time is more than money,

We find time to make new friends,
Time for ourselves and for others perfectly blends,

If a period of time disturbs you,
Positive-thinking helps to develop a proper view,

Don't rush with time!
Do things one- at- a- time!

57. Crab Curry Recipe

In Winter,
A culinary masterpiece;
Cooked with two-hands,
Delicious crab curry,
With deep savory flavors,
Mixture and consistency balance,
Stirring while staring,

Mouth- Watering delight,
Taste lingers,
Though cleaning the crab is a pain,
Appetizing is a gain,
Garnish the dish with love,
Enjoy a vibrant energy boost!

Recipe poem

58. Ollie- The Baby Elephant

You walk with the herd in the airy,
There's Ollie! I see your big belly,
You live in the grassland,
Not fitting in my land,
You are a brainy, roly-poly.

\# Limerick - Fun poem

59. An Art

An art creates beautiful imaginations,
An art expresses wonderful ideas and feelings,
An art is a combination of musical sounds and gestures,
An art is the movement of the feet,
An art is writing and reading,
An art is designing a broken ceramics glass,
An art is speech that is used wisely,
An art is to open a heart,
An art is to calm a violent situation.

Anaphora

60. A Splash

A splash
Is a quick dash..

A splash of water
On the face brings laughter..

A splash of all exquisite colors
Beautifies a painting...

A splash of lemonade
flavors the tongue...

A splash from a story
Stays in the memory...

A splash of good riddles
Is *plum-tickled...

A splash can stain
Or be unblemished and spotless...

*plum-tickled- being deeply happy

61. A fruitful tree

Tall Tree!
The litter fall
Utters the last whisper
Still dries to replenish then made
fruitful.

American cinquain

62. An Exceptionally Large Ocean

Loyal Love is vivid, enormous, unfathomable
like an ocean.
It shares an incredible view, WoW !

If only the ocean water is disturbed, it will form huge tidal waves.
That's the power of Loyal Love too!

There is always happiness,
contentment and satisfaction in exploring it.

How cool to feel an everlasting rhythm!
This is truly an exceptionally large ocean!

63. Struggles within

Struggles come my way
I don't underestimate it's peril
Struggles find it's own way
Struggles come my way
I feel stuck in a clay
I creep as a silkworm through the dark tunnel
Struggles come my way
I don't underestimate it's peril

#Triolet-ABa Aab AB

64. Yearning to be unlocked

The ones who are imprisoned
in their own weird thoughts;
yearn to pass through the railings
Any pleasant ideas or search for
a gap to find an outcome,
Through the wall of their
Unreal imaginations yet yearn:
For a trustworthy to open it's gate.

All over the empty still wall are
the self-sacrificing memories
Embossed, eyes roll in want,
There comes the hands that stretch
Wide to embrace,
Finally, their hearts are safely unlocked.

65. A Complete 100

The eyes look for the steadfast bond
because it knows the real value of love, trust
and treasures it in it's hidden beauty.

Inspiring, being thoughtful and affirmative
is like icing on the cake with tasty, lasting flavors of a dressed flower.

Even if seasons change or one is left in an empty desert
or feels ripped or wounded or dumped in a pit, the one can still
spread goodness valuing time to unlock a heart.

Enjoying in the pure rain in a park,
appreciating nature or standing in front of an ocean to feel the
rhythm of loyal love is the best satisfaction.

Indeed, it is worth the effort of a sibling:
The eyes may be filled with sorrowful or joyful tears.
A better meaningful life soon in PARADISE!

"Freestyle poetic thoughts" -are chosen from the 99 poems and
composed in brief to make a 100th one."

THE END